A Fisherman's Companion

A Fisherman's
Companion

ANTONY ATHA

HERMES
HOUSE

This edition published in 1997 by Hermes House
27 West 20th Street, New York, New York 10011

HERMES HOUSE books are available for bulk purchase for sales promotion and for premium use. For details, please write or call the manager of special sales, Hermes House, 27 West 20th Street, New York,
New York 10011; (800) 354-9657

© Anness Publishing Limited 1997

ISBN 1 901289 24 9

Publisher: Joanna Lorenz
Project Editor: Joanne Rippin
Designer: Prue Bucknall
Illustrator: Stephen Sweet

Printed and bound in Singapore

1 3 5 7 9 10 8 6 4 2

The following pictures are reproduced with the kind permission of:
ET Archive: 54b, *Thursday* by Walter Dendy Sadler, Tate Gallery, London. Fine Art Photographic: pp 2, *Trout Stream* by A A Glendening, Newman & Cooling Gallery; 7, *Young Boys Fishing in the Venetian Lagoon* by Antonio Paoletti; 9r, *Fishing* by Arthur Hunter; 25, *Fishing* by Francis Nys; 32-33, *The Fishing Expedition* by Henry John King courtesy of Bourne Gallery, Reigate; 35, *The Cardinal's Favourite Spot* by Jean Vibert; 36bl, *A Village Celebrity* by Walter Dendy Sadler; 50-51, *A Young Fisherman* by Henry John Yeend King; 53b, *Fishing on the Lake* by Charles Leslie courtesy of Beaton Brown Fine Painting, London; 57, *Fishing by Punt* by A W Redgate; Spectrum Colour Library: pp 12b; 16b; 34t; 37tl; 37tr; 38t; 38b; 39l; 39r; 40l; 40r; 41; 42l; 42r; 43; 52; 53t; 54t; 55; 56; 58. Visual Arts Library: pp 5, *Fishermen on the Banks of the River* by Gustave Doré; 8, *The Young Chinaman Fishing* by Anton Dorph, courtesy of Phillips Auctioneers; 10-11, *Watching the Float* by William Bromley; 59, *Le Ponte de Mantes* by Corot, Musée d'Orsay, Paris.

The publishers would like to thank publishers and copyright holders for permission to include the following copyright material: The Arthur Ransome Estate and Jonathan Cape Ltd for the extract from *Rod and Line*; the Estate of the Viscount Grey of Falloden, AP Watt Ltd (on behalf of Lady Irene Helen Graves) and Constable Publishers for the extracts from *Fly Fishing* and *The Falloden Papers*; David Higham Associates for the extract from *Confessions of a Carp Fisher* by "BB"; HarperCollins for the extracts from *A River Never Sleeps* by Roderick Haig Brown and the extract from *England Have My Bones* by TH White; Myfanwy Thomas and Faber and Faber Ltd for the extract from *The Childhood of Edward Thomas, a Fragment of Autobiography*.
The publishers have made every effort to trace all copyright holders of the quotations included in this book but if any necessary acknowledgements have been omitted we hope that the copyright holders will accept our apologies.

Contents

Introduction

...he that hopes to be a good Angler *must not only bring an inquiring, searching, observing wit; but he must bring a large measure of hope and patience, and a love and propensity to the Art itself; but having once got and practis'd it, then doubt not but* Angling *will prove to be so pleasant, that it will prove to be like Vertue,* a reward to it self.
IZAAK WALTON AND CHARLES COTTON
The Compleat Angler (1676 EDITION)

Many people come to fishing by accident rather than by design. If you come from a family of fishermen and women, it will be assumed that you want to fish, and father, mother, uncles and aunts will take you fishing with them. If you start fishing later, it will probably be through a friend. "I'm going fishing. Would you like to come?" could turn out to be the most important suggestion you ever receive.

Whatever you do, keep a fishing diary. If you are just starting out, you have ahead of you the most enjoyable days of your life. Write down what happens, even if it is just the bare statistics, and include the blank days. You will then have a record that will bring those hours back to you in the years to come.

days and successes he will no doubt recall, but always with the remembrance and the mind's vision of the scenes and the world in which he fished. For, indeed, this does seem a separate world, a world of beauty and enjoyment. The time must come to all of us who live long, when memory is more than prospect. An angler who has reached this stage and reviews the pleasure of life will be grateful and glad that he has been an angler, for he will look back on days radiant with happiness, peaks and peaks of enjoyment that are not less bright because they are lit in the memory by the light of the setting sun.
VISCOUNT GREY OF FALLODEN
Fly Fishing (1930 EDITION)

Thus, as the angler looks back he thinks less of individual captures and days than of the scenes in which he has fished. The luxuriance of water meadows, animated by insect and bird and trout life, tender with the green and gay with the blossoms of early spring: the nobleness and volume of great salmon rivers: the exhilaration of looking at any salmon pool, great or small; the rich brownness of Highland water: the wild openness of the treeless and trackless spaces which he has traversed in an explorer's spirit of adventure to search likely water for sea trout: now on one, now on another of these scenes an angler's mind will dwell, as he thinks of fishing. Special

OPPOSITE A painting showing young boys fishing in the Venetian lagoon by Antonio Paoletti, 1834–1912.

FIRST FISH

The first fish you catch, whether it be tench, roach or rudd, is the most precious one. That achievement can never be repeated and everyone will have their own cherished memory. But there is something extra special about your first Atlantic salmon. Catching that elusive fish produces a depth of feeling that is seldom found in any other form of sport. It is such a triumph, so totally unexpected, something no angler ever forgets.

He was on the bank! My first salmon. 10½ lbs. 13 minutes. Incredible but killed. I stuffed a pound into Macdonald's pocket, nearly cried and went on fishing. Occasionally I peeped at the salmon. For some reason I didn't like to give it a close look. It would have been a kind of hubris to look at it closely. It might have vanished.

T.H. WHITE

England Have My Bones (1936)

The best description of all is by Roland Pertwee in the short story *The River God.* The conclusion of that heroic drama is as satisfactory as it possibly could have been:

But I didn't break the cast. The noble, courageous, indomitable example of my river-god had lent me skill and precision beyond my years. When at long last a weary, beaten silvery monster rolled within reach of my arm into a shallow eddy, the steel gaff shot out fair and true, and sank home. And then I was lying on the grass, with my arms around a salmon that weighed twenty-two pounds on the scale and contained every sort of happiness known to a boy.

LEFT A painting of a young boy fishing by Anton Dorph, 1831–1914.

Not wedding days, nor schoolboy triumphs, nor student hopes fulfilled, nor snowy peaks, nor the hunter's fiercer joy will have so many cells in the honeycomb of memory as your first spring salmon.

A.H. CHAYTOR
Letters to a Salmon Fisher's Sons
(1910)

RIGHT A boy waits for a bite, in a work by Arthur Hunter, c1860.

The Fish

Enjoy thy streame, O harmless fish;
And when the angler, for his dish,
Through Gluttony's vile sin,
Attempts, a wretch, to pull thee out,
God give thee strength, O gentle trout,
To pull the rascall in!

PETER PINDAR

Ballad to a Fish of the Brooke (1816)

"Take my bait," cried Hiawatha,
Down into the depths beneath him,
"Take my bait, O Sturgeon, Nahma!
Come up from below the water,
Let us see which is the stronger!"

HENRY WADSWORTH LONGFELLOW

The Song of Hiawatha (1855)

OPPOSITE This dedicated young angler in a painting by William Bromley, 1835–88,
is likely to be luckier with the fish than in love.

ATLANTIC SALMON
(Salmo salar)

*T*he Atlantic salmon, the leaper, is an anadromous fish, that is it lives its adult life in saltwater but returns to freshwater to spawn. Almost all salmon return to the rivers where they were born; these rivers are found in many countries bordering the North Atlantic, ranging from Canada in the west to Iceland, Scotland, Ireland, Wales, Norway and Russia.

The adult salmon spawn in redds, depressions scraped in the gravel bed by the hen fish, and the eggs she releases are fertilized by the milt of the cock fish. Nearly all cock fish die after spawning but some 30 per cent of the females survive and return to the sea as kelts. The eggs hatch out into tiny creatures called alevins, which soon become fry and then turn into parr, small trout-like fish some 5–6 inches long with fingerprint markings down their sides.

Parr remain in the river for at least one and sometimes as long as five years and then, in May, they shed their trout-like colours and migrate to the sea as silvery smolts. When they reach the saltwater they travel up to the Greenland shelf, feeding voraciously and increasing rapidly in weight.

Atlantic salmon spend a variable amount of time at sea. They may return as grilse in the following June or July, weighing on average around 5–6 lbs after one winter at sea. If salmon spend two winters or more at sea, they may return to the river at any time of the year at weights ranging from 8–30 lbs, although some are much larger. Spawning takes place in November and December. Salmon stop feeding when they return to freshwater.

The salmon is anadromous. That is to say, he leads a double-life, one of them in freshwater, the other in saltwater. His freshwater life may be said to be his private, or love life; his saltwater life his ordinary, or workaday life. The salmon reverses the common order of human affairs: a lot is known about his private life but nothing at all about the rest. We get the chance to study him only when the salmon is making love.

WILLIAM HUMPHREY
The Spawning Run

The greatest of all sport in fly-fishing is that for spring salmon in a big river. It is in kind quite different from fly-fishing for trout. It is only by courtesy that the arrangement of feathers, especially on the huge hooks used in early spring, can be called a fly; and the motion of the fly in the water, carried round by the stream at the end of a long tight line, has no resemblance to that of any known insect; the fly works sunk in the water, and in spring is generally taken by the salmon without any break or sign on the surface of the water. What the angler expects is not a visible rise, but a sudden tightening of the line by a strong and undeniable pull. The sensation of this pull, especially if it comes after an hour or more of casting and unfulfilled expectation, is one of the great moments in the joy of life …

VISCOUNT GREY OF FALLODEN

Falloden Papers (1926)

TOP Painting of Atlantic salmon from *British Freshwater Fishes*
by Rev. W Houghton.
RIGHT *Salmo salar*, the leaper.
OPPOSITE Netting salmon at the mouth of a river.

PACIFIC SALMON
(Oncorhyncus)

These are the fish of the Pacific coast of North America. Much more plentiful than Atlantic salmon, there are five separate species with various names:

- ❖ Pink (*Oncorhyncus gorbuscha*), 2–5 lbs
- ❖ Sockeye or red (*Oncorhyncus nerka*), 6–12 lbs
- ❖ Silver or coho (*Oncorhyncus kisutch*), 12–14 lbs
- ❖ Chum or dog (*Oncorhyncus keta*), up to 20 lbs
- ❖ King, chinook or tyee (*Oncorhyncus tshawytscha*), up to 100 lbs or more

Pacific salmon spend their adult lives at sea, returning to the river to spawn. The pinks and the sockeye are the first to arrive. Around Bristol Bay in Alaska, 14 million sockeye move upstream in June and July. As they go, their silver bodies turn scarlet and their heads turn green. Next, in August, the coho run, followed by the chum and the king. Coho are the best fighting fish of all the Pacific salmon and readily take a fly.

O to break loose, like the Chinook salmon jumping and falling back,
nosing up the impossible stone and bone-crushing water fall —
raw-jawed, weak-fleshes there, stopped by ten steps of the roaring ladder,
and then to clear the top on the last try, alive enough to spawn and die.
ROBERT LOWELL
Waking Early Sunday Morning

Here in the four miles of the Campbell below Elk Falls, there are humpbacks and cutthroats that ran up in August. A touch of squaw winter, a three-day southeaster and heavy rain over Labor Day, will have brought the tyees through to the Canyon Pool. One sees them there a few days later, in the sunlight of an Indian summer, perhaps two or three hundred great, dark fish, square-tailed and thick-bodied, holding calmly midway between surface and bottom in ten or twenty feet of transparent green water. I always look among them for a real giant, but I have not seen him yet ... Nothing is more impressive than the sight of a big school of tyees under the smooth surface of the Canyon Pool in September. They are so big and calm and dignified, so clearly visible, so solidly set in their still-distant spawning purpose, so utterly contemptuous of a fly or spoon drawn across them or among them. And they have lost none of their ocean perfection. They are dark, it is true, but their bodies are perfect, thick across the back, tremendously powerful.
RODERICK HAIG-BROWN
A River Never Sleeps (1948)

TOP Chinook salmon.
ABOVE Coho salmon.

BROWN TROUT
(Salmo trutta fario)

SEA TROUT
(Salmo trutta trutta)

Indigenous to northern Europe, the brown trout has been successfully introduced to most countries of the world, including the United States. Some of the best trout fishing is to be found in New Zealand and Tasmania and writers have long extolled the joys of fishing the famous chalk streams of southern England.

The life cycle of brown trout is the same as that of the salmon except that they do not migrate to the sea. They live in a wide variety of habitats, from rivers and streams to lakes and lochs, but, like all trout, require running water to spawn.

Trout feed on insects, including mayflies (Ephemeroptera), and small fish, and the trout fisherman has to imitate this food if he or she is to be successful.

He was the most beautiful trout I had ever seen. Not quite two pounds, but hugely thick and short and deep, with a tiny head and a huge tail. His back was a rich, deep olive, his belly pale golden, his red spots were big and vivid, and over his whole side was a sheen of red, a diffusion rather than an overlaid color, the golden redness of sunset light.

RODERICK HAIG-BROWN

A River Never Sleeps (1948)

TOP Brown trout.
TOP RIGHT Sea trout.

There is no real physiological difference between sea trout and brown trout, although sea trout from the sea are silver in colour, and both are classified as *Salmo trutta*. The difference lies in their behaviour. Sea trout, like salmon, migrate to the sea as smolts. Generally they do not journey too far from the rivers of their birth and all sea trout return to spawn after one winter at sea. The whole sea trout population of a river therefore enters the river in one year, unlike salmon, and this makes them very vulnerable to fungus diseases such as ulcerative dermal necrosis (UDN).

Sea trout like still water and the ideal sea-trout fishery is a lake or loch connected to the sea by a short river. There are a number of these to be found on the west coast of Scotland and Ireland as well as in the northeast United States. Sea trout continue to feed in freshwater but, unlike brown trout, they feed spasmodically and are usually caught on flies that imitate small fish or lures.

Quick and yet he moves like silk. I envy dreams that see his curving silver in the weeds. When stiff as snags he blends with certain stones. When evening pulls the ceiling tight across his back he leaps for bugs.

RICHARD HUGO

Trout

RAINBOW TROUT
(Oncorhyncus mykiss, Salmo gairdneri)

Rainbow trout, so called after the broad pink stripe down their sides, are native to the rivers of the west coast of America from the Bering Strait down to the Gulf of California. There they share ancestry with the Pacific salmon and are classified with that group. They are also to be found in Russia and as far south as the Chinese border. In Europe the rainbow trout, introduced from North America, is a universally successful stock and farmed fish, classified with the *Salmo* group.

In their native waters, rainbows will migrate to the sea where they can, returning as steelheads, the Pacific sea trout. They go to sea to feed and only the larger fish return. Big runs of steelhead enter the rivers in autumn and winter to spawn in late winter and early spring. Gradually they take on the colours of the rainbows that remained in the rivers until the only difference is their size. These are unpredictable, fighting fish often caught on the fly. Nearly all the European rainbows are bred in captivity, although there are a few rivers where they breed successfully. They are caught in man-made lakes and reservoirs in the same way as brown trout, though they swim in shoals and are often taken on lures fished very deep. They are generally less discriminating than brown trout.

RIGHT Playing a trout in the height of summer.

CUTTHROAT
(Oncorhyncus clarki, Salmo clarki)

Cutthroats are a species of trout native to western America and the Rocky Mountains. Those living in the west coast rivers from Alaska to northern California migrate to the sea to feed. They don't venture far and after just a few months return to freshwater in great numbers in the late summer. They are usually caught on a fly.

Some cutthroats stay in freshwater all their lives and these tend to inhabit the cold headwaters, though their numbers are dwindling.

Apart from the two red throat marks under the lower jaw, cutthroats vary in colour and size but they are not large fish.

ARCTIC CHAR
(Salvelinus alpinus)

The Arctic char lives in the rivers of northern Europe as a sea-going fish that returns to the rivers to spawn. It can also be found as a land-locked species in lakes of Europe, Asia and North America. It survives in Britain in the Lake District and in some lochs in Scotland where they are usually caught trolling. Some Irish and Alpine lakes also support good populations. In North America, they are found in the northern reaches of New England and range northward through Canada, Alaska and the Aleutian Islands.

BROOK TROUT
(Salvelinus fontinalis)

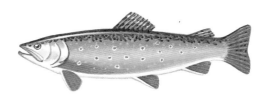

A native of eastern North America, the brook trout lives in cold, clear, fast-flowing streams. Once abundant throughout this region, the steady encroachment of civilization has taken quite a toll on fisheries. The brook trout has recently been introduced into Europe as a fish that will survive in lowland waters, where it is used as a stock fish but it is less discriminating and not so wily as the native brown trout.

ABOVE A dry fly fisherman casting upstream. Dusk is a good time to try an artificial sedge in these pools for the larger trout.

GRAYLING
(*Thymallus thymallus, Thymallus arcticus*)

The Grayling is called in Latin Thymalus, a Thymo having a scent like the flowers of thyme.
ROBIN HOWLETT
The Angler's Sure Guide (1706)

The grayling have bright silver scales with a number of horizontal stripes, purple in colour, along their flanks. Their most prominent feature is their giant orange-brown dorsal fin. The grayling is widely distributed in northern Europe. It is less common in North America but is nevertheless a highly prized fish of both lakes and rivers. The grayling is a relation of the salmon, but it spawns in the spring rather than the winter. Grayling are at their best in the autumn and, while they are not popular on the chalkstreams, on other rivers they are a much sought-after quarry. They are generally caught on artificial flies.

WHITEFISH
(*Coregonus laveratus spp.*)

There are a number of local species, minor members of the Salmonidae family, that are found in Great Britain and North America. The mountain whitefish is found in the rivers of Montana where it lives as a shoal fish running as large as 3 lbs. They are all silvery with longish scales and an adipose fin. All European whitefish are thought to come from the houting, which is a sea-going fish mainly found in the Baltic. Gwyniad are found in some lakes in Wales, powan in Loch Lomond in Scotland and vendace (*Coregonus albula*) in Lough Neagh. They can provide good sport on the fly, but they are not very sought after by game fishermen. Generally, whitefish are in decline in European waters.

ABOVE Vendace (top), grayling and gwyniad. Vendace and gwyniad are both whitefish. Gwyniad are found in Wales and vendace in Lough Neagh in Northern Ireland.

BARBEL
(Barbus barbus)

Barbel are bronze-green in colour with strong muscular bodies and four barbules, much sought after as a quarry. They are powerful fish that live in fast-flowing rivers where they are adapted to feeding on the bottom. The Hampshire Avon is the best-known barbel fishery in Britain and the River Thames used to be a famous river for barbel. They can be caught on a number of baits, including maggots, cheese, processed meat and worms. They need heavy tackle as they run large and are powerful fighters.

BLEAK
(Alburnus alburnus)

Bleak are small silver fish that live in rivers, although they have been introduced to some stillwaters. Surface feeders, bleak swim in shoals and can be caught on a fly as well as paste or maggots.

BREAM, BLUEGILLS
(Abramis brama)

One of the most common fish in Britain and Europe, the common, or bronze, bream lives in large shoals. Adult bream have deep brown backs, bronze sides and cream-coloured bellies. They often feed in deep silt and can be located by the muddying of the river near where they are feeding. Bream can grow to a great size and will accept most baits, from sweetcorn and paste to bread and maggots. The silver bream, *(Blicca bjoerkna)*, found throughout Europe, is a more delicate fish and never grows as big as the common bream. It has grey fins with silver scales.

ABOVE Pomeranian bream and white or silver bream, mainly found in Europe.

CARP
(*Cyprinus carpio*)

The common carp has a purple back, golden-yellow sides and a cream belly. It comes from China but has existed in the west for centuries. It was the most commonly stocked fish in the stew ponds of medieval monasteries. Common carp are fully scaled, mirror carp have few scales along the lateral lines, and leather carp are scaleless. Carp fishing is a form of religion and requires a dedication and skill that is not found in any other form of angling.

In one Day we caught about twenty brace of extraordinary large Carps with very sweet Eeles and Tench; I believe I shall hardly forget the Pearch of eighteen inches long, caught by Capt. Comer, nor the Old Gentleman's resolution, while we were drinking a Dram of the Bottle, a Fish run with his rod, which he being unwilling to loose, stript off his Cloaths and leapt in, and in swimming proved too nimble for the Fish, for I assure you, he brought them both out with much content to regain his Rod.

JOHN WHITNEY
The Dedication to The Genteel Recreation: Or the Pleasure of Angling, A Poem (1700)

ABOVE A common carp (below) with an orfe and koi carp above. The domestic goldfish is another member of the carp family.

CRAPPIE
(*Pomoxis nigromaculatus, Pomoxis annularis*)

Black and white crappies are found in large numbers in North America, from Canada to Mexico and as far east as New York and as far west as the Great Plains. The crappie thrives anywhere where food is plentiful. This less than discriminating fish provides lots of excitement for young anglers who are just learning the joys of fishing and is excellent eating.

CHUB
(*Leuciscus cephalus*)

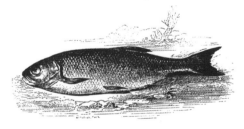

The chub is a thickset fish with a blackish back, silvery sides and creamy belly that lives in rivers. They prefer clean water with a constant flow over a gravel or sandy bottom. They can be caught on a number of baits from flies to luncheon meat, sweetcorn and maggots, and are sometimes indiscriminate in their feeding.

DACE
(Leuciscus leuciscus)

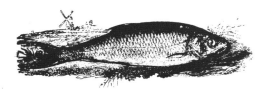

*D*ace live in fast-flowing streams and have earned themselves the nickname "darter" for their dashing habits. Like roach, they are shoal fish, although they are smaller and seldom reach more than ¾ lb. They feed on invertebrates and also take nymphs and flies. They have greenish-black backs and silvery sides with white bellies.

GUDGEON
(Gobio gobio)

*G*udgeon live in slow-moving rivers with gravelly bottoms and are similar to barbel in having two tusks. They are very small fish, a gudgeon of 4 oz is a triumph, and they are often caught by young anglers. They feed on the bottom favouring insect larvae and freshwater shrimps. They are an attractive fish with a greeny brown back fading to yellow on the belly.

I fished with a worm either tied on the cotton line or impaled on a bent pin and put my stickleback or my rare lovely spotted gudgeon in a glass jam-jar.
EDWARD THOMAS
The Childhood of Edward Thomas, a Fragment of Autobiography (1938)

EELS
(Anguilla anguilla)

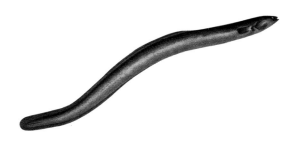

*E*els are the most romantic of creatures and breed several thousands of miles away in the Sargasso Sea. They journey to Europe, floating on the Gulf Stream as creatures that look like transparent leaves. After three or four years they arrive in Europe where they change their shape and become longer and thinner when they are known as elvers. Elvers travel upstream in the same way as salmon. A male eel will spend up to 10 years in freshwater, while female eels spend as long as 19 years. Then they return to the Sargasso Sea to spawn and die.

As the eels prepare for the migration back to their spawning-grounds, they become black on the back with silver flanks. The eyes enlarge and the jaws take on a pointed shape, possibly due to the eel's lack of need to continue feeding while on the breeding journey. Both elvers and adult eels will migrate across land, between watercourses and enclosed stillwaters that have no connecting streams. After periods of heavy rainfall, when this usually takes place, there is sufficient moisture for the eels to wriggle across fields and even roads. Eels inhabit rivers, ponds and lakes and are often caught on a worm. They make delicious eating.

LARGEMOUTH BASS
(*Micropterus salmoides*)

This is the most popular North American sporting fish and has been introduced to Europe where it is becoming more common. Largemouth bass can be caught on flies but are most frequently caught spinning, and the plug is the most popular bait. They require weedy shallow water of above 17°C/62°F.

When compared to a cold trout stream, a healthy bass pond is as rich as a
jungle, a stew of life so thick you can almost walk on it by midsummer,
and a successful largemouth bass will eat anything that
isn't big enough to eat him first.
JOHN GIERACH
Trout Bum

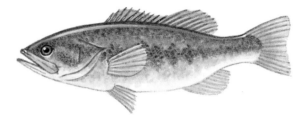

Folklore has it that upon hearing the clicking of the reel, a fish will rise to the top to snatch the "insect" that awaits him.

From ebery nook en connor
Natur's mel'dies roun' me steal
But nun ob dem am in it
Wid de clickin' ob de reel.
ANON
De Clickin' ob de Reel (nineteenth century)

PERCH
(*Perca fluviatilis*)

Perch live in many waters throughout Europe. They are handsome fish with sharply spined dorsal fins, greenish-black sides, white bellies and bright orange fins. They also have prominent blackish bars down their sides. They are predators like pike but hunt in shoals. A favourite quarry of young fishermen, they are very good to eat but rather bony.

The bright-eyed perch with fins of Tyrian dye;
The silver eel, in shining volumes roll'd;
The yellow carp, in scales bedropp'd with gold;
Swift trouts, diversified with crimson stains;
And Pikes, the tyrants of the watery plains.
ALEXANDER POPE
Windsor Forest (1713)

PIKE
(Esox lucius)

The Pike is a melancholy Fish, swims by himself and lives alone.

ROBERT HOWLETT

The Angler's Sure Guide: or Angling Improved (1706)

The "tyrant of the river", pike exist as solitary predators in many waters throughout Europe and North America. Pike eat live and dead fish, water mammals and birds and are caught by live bait, spinning and dead-baiting. The best pike fishing is in the winter. Pike grow to a large size, but all the largest fish are females with the males hardly ever reaching more than 10 lbs. Female fish from 45–50 lbs have been recorded in various waters around Britain. They are handsome fish with green-bronze upper bodies and creamy white bellies. They have ferocious teeth; you must always fish with a wire trace, and a disgorger is essential.

ABOVE Pike fishing on the River Lea, Chingford, England.

ROACH
(Rutilus rutilus)

There bent in hopeful musings on the brink
They watch their floating corks that seldom sink,
Save when a wary roach or silver bream
Nibbles the worm as passing up the stream,
Just urging expectation's hopes to stay
To view the dodging cork, then slink away.

JOHN CLARE

Rustic Fishing (1821)

Roach are widely distributed in Europe and are found in many rivers and stillwaters. They are brightly coloured fish with silvery sides and reddish fins. They are much sought after as a quarry and can be caught on a wide range of baits, but are very delicate and shy feeders with tiny suspicious mouths and are exceedingly difficult to hook – striking is the art of roach fishing. They live in shoals and spawn in the spring.

RUDD
(Scardinius erythrophthalmus)

Rudd are widely distributed in Europe and prefer stillwater. They are a very beautiful fish with golden sides and red fins. They live in shoals and can be caught on most baits.

ABOVE Azurine, dobule and rudd

SMALLMOUTH BASS
(Micropterus punctulatus)

This highly prized North American sport fish is native to the eastern half of the United States and southeastern Canada. The smallmouth thrives in cool, clean rivers with gravelly bottoms and deep rocky lakes. It has a golden bronze back with a cream-coloured belly and dark vertical marks or bands on its flanks. It can be identified by a jaw that extends directly below the eye.

TENCH
(Tinca tinca)

The tench has an olive-green back shading to a golden belly. It is a summer fish and is associated with the opening days of the coarse fishing season in June. The classic way to catch tench is by raking the swim. Paste and sweetcorn baits are favoured.

WALLEYE
(Stizostedion vitreum)

Named for its large, glassy, opaque eyes, the walleye is one of the most sought-after sport fish in North America. They strike readily on jigs tipped with live minnows, night crawlers, and leeches, as well as small yellow plastic grubs and salamanders fished on the bottom.

OPPOSITE *Fishing* by Francis Nys (1863-1900).

FISHING RECORDS

DATE ....

WATER ....

RODS ....

WEATHER ....

    AIR TEMPERATURE .... WATER TEMPERATURE ....

    CONDITIONS ....

    WIND DIRECTION ....

THE CATCH

FISH ....

....

WEIGHT ....

HOW CAUGHT ....

COMMENTS ....

....

....

DATE ....

WATER ....

RODS ....

WEATHER ....

    AIR TEMPERATURE .... WATER TEMPERATURE ....

    CONDITIONS ....

    WIND DIRECTION ....

THE CATCH

FISH ....

....

WEIGHT ....

HOW CAUGHT ....

COMMENTS ....

....

....

FISHING RECORDS

DATE ....

WATER ....

RODS ....

WEATHER ....

    AIR TEMPERATURE .... WATER TEMPERATURE ....

    CONDITIONS ....

    WIND DIRECTION ....

THE CATCH

FISH ....

....

WEIGHT ....

HOW CAUGHT ....

COMMENTS ....

....

....

....

DATE ....

WATER ....

RODS ....

WEATHER ....

    AIR TEMPERATURE .... WATER TEMPERATURE ....

    CONDITIONS ....

    WIND DIRECTION ....

THE CATCH

FISH ....

....

WEIGHT ....

HOW CAUGHT ....

COMMENTS ....

....

....

FISHING RECORDS

DATE ....

WATER ....

RODS ....

WEATHER ....

     AIR TEMPERATURE .... WATER TEMPERATURE ....

     CONDITIONS ....

     WIND DIRECTION ....

THE CATCH

FISH ....

....

WEIGHT ....

HOW CAUGHT ....

              COMMENTS ....

....

....

DATE ....

WATER ....

RODS ....

WEATHER ....

     AIR TEMPERATURE .... WATER TEMPERATURE ....

     CONDITIONS ....

     WIND DIRECTION ....

THE CATCH

FISH ....

....

WEIGHT ....

HOW CAUGHT ....

COMMENTS ....

....

....

....

FISHING RECORDS

DATE ....

WATER ....

RODS ....

WEATHER ....

    AIR TEMPERATURE .... WATER TEMPERATURE ....

    CONDITIONS ....

    WIND DIRECTION ....

THE CATCH

FISH ....

....

WEIGHT ....

HOW CAUGHT ....

COMMENTS ....

....

....

DATE ....

WATER ....

RODS ....

WEATHER ....

    AIR TEMPERATURE .... WATER TEMPERATURE ....

    CONDITIONS ....

    WIND DIRECTION ....

THE CATCH

FISH ....

....

WEIGHT ....

HOW CAUGHT ....

COMMENTS ....

....

....

A Fisherman's Companion

FISHING RECORDS

DATE ....

WATER ....

RODS ....

WEATHER ....

    AIR TEMPERATURE .... WATER TEMPERATURE ....

    CONDITIONS ....

    WIND DIRECTION ....

THE CATCH

FISH ....

....

WEIGHT ....

HOW CAUGHT ....

COMMENTS ....

....

....

DATE ....

WATER ....

RODS ....

WEATHER ....

    AIR TEMPERATURE .... WATER TEMPERATURE ....

    CONDITIONS ....

    WIND DIRECTION ....

THE CATCH

FISH ....

....

WEIGHT ....

HOW CAUGHT ....

COMMENTS ....

....

....

FISHING RECORDS

DATE ....

WATER ....

RODS ....

WEATHER ....

    AIR TEMPERATURE .... WATER TEMPERATURE ....

    CONDITIONS ....

    WIND DIRECTION ....

THE CATCH

FISH ....

....

WEIGHT ....

HOW CAUGHT ....

COMMENTS ....

....

....

DATE ....

WATER ....

RODS ....

WEATHER ....

    AIR TEMPERATURE .... WATER TEMPERATURE ....

    CONDITIONS ....

    WIND DIRECTION ....

THE CATCH

FISH ....

....

WEIGHT ....

HOW CAUGHT ....

COMMENTS ....

....

....

Tackle and Techniques

Whenever you go out to Fish, faill not to have with you, viz. A good Coat for all Weathers. An Apron to put your Ground-Bait, Stones, and Paste in. A Basket to put your Fish in. A neat Rod of about four Foot long, in several pieces, one with another. Two or three Lines fitted up, of all Sorts. Spare Hooks, Links, Floats, Silk, Wax, Plummetts, Caps, and a Landing Nett, etc. And if you have a boy to go along with you, a good Neats-Tongue, and a Bottle of Canary should not be wanting.

WILLIAM GILBERT

Gilbert's Delight (1676)

OPPOSITE *The Fishing Expedition* by Henry John Yeend King, 1855-1924.

WHAT TO TAKE

Whenever you go fishing you must take with you your rod, reel, line, nylon for casts, hooks, bait and float. This is the minimum.

Of these items the reel, line, nylon and hooks are the most important. If you forget your rod, you can cut a branch from a tree; if you forget your bait, you can look for worms under stones or cowpats; if you forget your flies and you are an habitual fly fisherman, there may be one or two stuck in your hat or your jacket which will serve.

Nets are important, but not that important. If you hook a fish and you have no net, there is usually some way of getting it out of the water; although I would always take a net when fishing from a boat.

The equipment you take depends very much on the scale of the expedition and the quarry you are after. Competing in a challenge match requires a number of rods, floats, different-sized hooks, various baits, stools, keep nets, spare reels and groundbait. Two hours on your home water fishing for trout probably only requires rod, reel,

a roll of nylon for a spare cast and a box of flies.

You will have more chance of success if you are properly equipped. Take a range of baits and a large choice of flies. Take nylon of various weights. If you are fishing new waters, find out in advance the likely weight of fish.

There are rods of every type and description. Try out a new rod before you buy it. Different waters require different rods; a small overgrown trout stream in Wales may require a rod no longer than 5 feet, while most North American trout streams require a fly rod of 8 to 8½ feet, and a Norwegian salmon river requires a fly rod of 18 feet. Always buy the best equipment you can afford, particularly reels which receive far more wear and tear than any other item of equipment. Look after your reels; dry and oil them at the end of the season.

TOP A modern trout reel by Sharpe's of Aberdeen.
ABOVE A Nottingham reel.
BOTTOM An old-fashioned creel and fish from a nineteenth-century engraving.

TOP RIGHT A rod rack outside an Irish fishing hotel with kettles.
OPPOSITE *The Cardinal's Favourite Spot* by Jean Vibert, 1840-1902.

TIPS ON TACKLE

● Renew your nylon every year. Throw away the old spools. If you don't, write the year of purchase on the spool. Do not be too surprised when the large fish you have just hooked breaks you if you are fishing with five-year-old line.

● Wind a new line carefully on to the reel under slight tension. This prevents loose coils, which can bite into one another and jam the reel when you have just hooked that very large fish.

● Salmon and trout fishermen should walk to the river trailing the whole length of a new fly line through the grass behind them. It is a good idea to walk like this for at least a quarter of a mile. It removes any kinks in the new line.

● Hooks should be sharp. Keep a hook sharpener in your fishing bag.

● Nets should be as large as is convenient. A solid rim is essential. Never buy a net with a soft loop of leather or twine at the front. Check your net every once in a while in case holes have been torn in it through which a fish might fall.

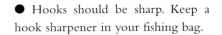

● Scissors and disgorgers are important but not essential unless you are fishing for pike. Then you also need one or two pairs of forceps, at least 8 inches long. For other fish, fishing scissors with square blunt ends are enormously helpful for extracting hooks.

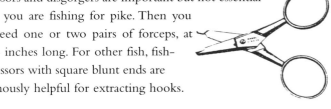

ABOVE *A Village Celebrity* by Walter Dendy Sadler, 1854–1923.

TOP LEFT & CENTRE RIGHT Modern rods and reels are light, efficient and powerful. LINE ENGRAVINGS Knife, disgorger and scissors from *Hardy's Angler's Guides* of 1934 and 1937.

CASTING

*A*ll fishermen have to learn to cast. The coarse fisherman has to lay out his tackle in position in the swim, the salmon fisher has to place his fly or minnow as far and exactly as possible across a river and the dry fly fisherman has to put his fly alongside the nose of the rising trout.

The elements of casting are simple. You use the rod to throw the line across the water, at the end of which is a leader or cast and your lure.

If you are casting a bait, start with a short line and swing the bait out overhead, underarm or sideways; the weight of the bait carries it across the water and the line runs out from the reel – either a fixed spool or a multiplier – both of which allow the line to run out without friction. With practice, most anglers achieve a fair proficiency. An expert can achieve miracles of distance and accuracy.

Fishing the River Spey, an overhead cast.

The end of a Spey or roll cast.

Casting a fly, wet or dry, with a trout or salmon rod is rather more difficult but the essential elements are much the same. The angler has to use the balance and power of the rod to throw the line and fly across the water. This is done in a rhythm that allows the fly to extend behind the angler and then propels it forward. Casting well requires practice and any keen fly fisherman should practise on a lawn aiming at a plate on the grass, trying to make the fly land as lightly as possible.

RIGHT & ABOVE Illustrations of casting from *Dry Fly Fishing in Theory and Practice* by F. M. Halford.

CASTING TIPS

● Don't take the rod back too far, try not to let it go past the vertical and you will get it about right.
● Don't be frightened of making the rod bend; use more force when taking the fly back than when pushing it forward.
● Let the fly extend behind you and pause at the top of the cast: up two, three – down.
● Practise. As you become more experienced, so you will become more proficient.

FISHING METHODS

FLY FISHING

Fishing with a fly is the best way to catch salmon, trout and grayling.

In dry-fly fishing, a representation of the natural insect is cast upstream and allowed to float down on the surface film over a feeding fish that you can see rising. You hope the fish will be deceived into mistaking the artificial fly for the natural. In small, fast-flowing streams, trout will move very quickly to the fly, and often the difficulty is to strike quickly enough to hook them. On slow-moving streams the converse is true; fish move gently to the fly and the difficulty is to strike slowly enough.

In nymph fishing, the angler is trying to imitate the nymph as it rises to the surface of the river. The nymph is fished underwater and you have to anticipate the take by watching the end of your leader – if it stops, strike. Sometimes you will see a fish turn in the water by your fly and again you have to strike. Sometimes your nymph will be so close to the surface that you will see the movement as a rise form. Nymph fishing at this level is supremely difficult and requires a great concentration, knowledge of the river and of the insects the trout are likely to be feeding on.

Wet-fly fishing is practised in many rivers and stillwaters, generally with three, sometimes four, flies on a cast. These can either be fished downstream, when the current pulls the flies round in an arc, or up and across. The flies will usually represent nymphs and the fisherman should fish all the likely spots in the river, letting his flies swim over rocks and down the banks. In stillwaters, the fisherman creates movement by working the flies back towards him either towards the bank or the boat. The traditional lake-style fishing from a boat, casting a shortish line with a longish rod and working the top fly to the surface of the water where it bobs along the tops of the waves, can be very successful not only for trout but also for sea trout.

Dapping on lakes or stillwaters is another form of fly fishing. A light floss line blows out in front of the boat, and the angler bounces a large fly such as a Daddy Longlegs on the top of the water. This can be a deadly method for sea trout and trout.

In salmon fishing, the fisherman aims to fish a fly over the lie in as controlled a manner as possible. This means casting downstream at an angle and letting the fly come round in an arc in the same way as the traditional wet fly. The salmon fisher is trying to stimulate the feeding instinct of the salmon and the best way to do this is by making the fly behave like a small fish, swimming erratically across the current. Keep the line straight and pull the fly towards you a few inches at a time. In the summer, fish the fly more slowly than early in the year.

TOP Wet fly fishing in summer, River Ribble, Lancashire, England.
BELOW A float beside a reed bed.

FLOAT FISHING

In float fishing, the float swims on the top of the water with the bait suspended below it. This is the most effective way of presenting bait to the fish, and there are a wide variety of floats available to suit different waters and conditions. It is one of the most exciting moments in all angling when the float twitches and then slides away beneath the water, pulled under by the unseen fish that may prove the capture of a lifetime. Among the most popular floats are the Avon floats, developed for the fast waters of the river Avon, the Drennan loafer, stick floats, balsas and wagglers. Some floats are designed to lift when a fish takes the bait from the bottom so that you strike when the tip of the float rises.

Fishing techniques are many and varied. Being able to adapt to the river conditions at the time is the key.

SPINNING OR BAIT-CASTING

A spun bait can catch salmon, trout, sea trout, perch, pike and zander or walleye. When you are spinning you are imitating a small fish, and therefore, this method of fishing works well for the predatory species. The bait can be spun upstream or downstream and the experienced angler will be able to explore all the likely lies in his water. You can spin with a mounted small fish, but the most-used spinning baits are artificial minnows, spoons and plugs.

LEGERING, JIGGING OR BOTTOM FISHING

ABOVE Fishing the lake in Epping Forest, near London.

Legering, or jigging, with a running leger, paternoster, or bottom-fishing jig is the time-honoured method of holding a bait at the bottom of the river or lake. The angler is in direct contact with his bait and bites are registered at the quivertip of the rod or felt by hand. A bottom-fishing rig holds the bait in one position in the water and the depth is irrelevant.

ABOVE Angling on a peaceful river bank can be very relaxing.

FLIES AND FLY FISHING

The jealous trout that low did lie,
Rose at a well-dissembled flie;
HENRY WOTTON
On a Bank as I Sate A-fishing (1651)

Trout fishing is the angler's ultimate pleasure. Trout feed on insects, and the successful fisherman is the one who accurately imitates the fly on which the fish are feeding. At its most exacting this means casting a concoction of feathers and thread, tied to imitate a natural insect, to a fish in clear water, so lightly and accurately that the fish is deceived into taking it.

This applies to stillwater anglers just as much as to the purest dry fly fisherman on the chalkstreams of southern England or the spring-fed streams of Pennsylvania, though some may disagree. Many anglers claim that the best flies for rainbow trout, particularly in stillwaters and reservoirs, are lures of various shapes and sizes. Well, yes, a large number of fish are caught on gaudy creations, but many of these represent small fish or the larvae of dragon- or damselflies. Rainbow trout can be induced to attack a lure, but if you always fish with an imitation of the fly on which the trout are feeding, in the long run you will catch more. A little bit of thought can make a big difference.

ABOVE Fly-tiers table.
RIGHT Grayling fishing on the River Lambourn, one of the chalkstreams of southern England.

Rivers are different. There you can often see the fish, and if you can't see the fish, you can usually see the flies they are feeding on. The most important flies for the angler to know about are the Ephemeroptera, the mayflies or olives, which are water-borne flies with folded upright wings. In Britain the name mayfly is used specifically for the *Ephemera danica,* which hatches in May.

As they hatch ephemeroptera go through three stages, all of which are of interest to the fisherman. The eggs, laid on the surface

Doubt not but that Angling is an Art; is it not an Art to deceive a Trout with an artificial Flie? a Trout! that is more sharp sighted than any Hawk you have nam'd, and more watchful and timorous than your high mettled Marlin is bold?
IZAAK WALTON AND CHARLES COTTON
The Compleat Angler (1676 EDITION)

ABOVE Tying on a new fly.

of the water, sink to the bottom and attach themselves to weed or stones. They hatch out into small nymphs, which live on the river bed until they mature, when they rise up to the surface of the water. Trout feed on the nymphs as they rise. To catch a trout on a representation of the nymph on which it feeds is the summit of the angler's art. Anglers fishing with wet flies on fast-flowing streams are seeking trout feeding on nymphs and many of the best-known old wet fly patterns are representations of nymphs.

On reaching the surface the nymph changes into the dun, or sub-imago. The wings emerge and the fly floats down river on the surface. At this stage they can be seen clearly by trout and angler. The hatch, or rise, is the moment that all fishermen wait for. All you have to do is identify what type of mayfly the trout are taking, tie on a good representation and cast lightly and accurately. In practice it isn't quite as easy as it sounds!

The final stage of the mayfly's life is its transformation into the imago, the fully mature fly. After mating the female returns to the river to lay her eggs and then dies. She floats downstream, sometimes half submerged, with her wings outstretched like a cross. Trout most often feed on these spent flies or spinners in the evening. Male spinners are found but they are of less interest to the feeding trout.

MOST USEFUL WET FLIES AND NYMPHS	
FOR RIVERS	Snipe and Purple: a representation of the iron blue nymph Greenwell's Glory: a general representation of the olive nymph Pheasant Tail Partridge and Orange Blae and Black: good in May when the hawthorn fly is hatching Hare's Ear: a representation of the hatching olive March Brown Green Drake Zug Bug Leadwing Coachman Stonefly
FOR LAKES AND LOCHS	Blue Zulu Invicta Soldier Palmer Coch y bhondu Heather Sedge Buzzer Nymph
FOR STILLWATERS	Buzzer Nymphs: representations of midge larvae Corixa: representations of water beetles Damselfly Nymphs

MOST USEFUL DRY FLIES
Iron Blue Dun Olive Quill Black Gnat Cahill Hendrickson Quill Gordon Royal Coachman White Wulff Kite's Imperial Any Mayfly during the mayfly hatch

SALMON FISHING

Salmon fishing, one of the greatest of all sports, is beset by chance, luck and disaster. As salmon do not feed when they are in freshwater, the salmon fisherman has to try to stimulate the feeding instinct from the days when the salmon was a parr in the river during its infancy or at sea, feeding on small fish and plankton. Certain water and weather conditions are more favourable to this than others. Salmon can be caught on a bait, usually a worm, shrimp or prawn, or artificial minnows and flies.

Salmon flies are completely different from trout flies. The size of the fly is far more important than the pattern and many experienced salmon fishermen have fished the whole year with just one pattern for a bet. Most salmon fishermen have favourite patterns that they stick to, but it is a good idea to take local advice when fishing new water.

The warmer the water is, the smaller the fly. Most salmon fishermen make the mistake of fishing with flies that are too large.

RECOMMENDED SALMON FLIES

Stoat's Tail and Silver Stoat's Tail
Tadpole
Black and Yellow
Shrimp
Willie Gunn
plus in the summer:
Hairy Mary
Blue Charm
Black Bomber
Black Wulff
Jock Scott
Red Butt
Cooseboom
Butterfly

Fly fishing for salmon in the fast-flowing rivers of Iceland, Scotland, Norway and Russia is the peak of the salmon fisher's art.

Salmon flies have changed, though. There was a time when flies were beautiful concoctions composed of many exotic feathers. Their names matched their beauty and embellished the romance of salmon fishing: "I captured my best salmon with a Green Highlander", you could say, or "It fell for Lady Caroline". Nowadays flies are plainer and have less romance.

ABOVE LEFT Old fashioned salmon flies.
BELOW Fly fishing for salmon on a river in the Highlands, Scotland.

BAITS

The Worm as a Bait

And with this baite hath often taken been
The salmon fair of river fish the best;
The Shad that in the spring time cometh in,
The Suant swift, that is not set by least,
The Bocher sweet, the pleasant Flounder thin,
The Peele the tweate, The Batling and the rest;
With many more that in the deep doe lye
of Avon, Uske, of Severne, and of Wye.

JOHN DENNYS
The Secrets of Angling (1613)

There are as many baits as anglers have imagination to think of them. It all depends on what the fish will take on that particular day. Ideally the fisherman should spend some time just observing but, failing that, it is possible to catch almost every species of freshwater fish on a worm or maggot. The only exceptions are predatory fish – pike, catfish and zander or walleye, which prefer deadbaits such as smelts or pieces of herring. Other natural baits include slugs, crayfish and shrimp.

Breadcrust and bread flake, luncheon meat and cheese paste have all proved to be deadly, and particle baits are now well-established. These must always be soaked and/or boiled before use. They are also useful for groundbaiting. They include hempseed, sweetcorn, peanuts, black-eyed peas, tares, maple peas, sinking trout pellets, and even dog biscuits.

Different fish show preferences for certain food. Barbel often find a bunch of maggots irresistible, chub are partial to bread and slugs, carp are fond of bread paste mixed with honey, lumps of cheese and boilies and have even been tempted by a dried dog biscuit cast over them as a dry fly.

Groundbaiting is part of the art of angling and it is a skill that has to be learned. The purpose is to attract fish into your swim and to stimulate their appetites. Proprietary mixes are available from tackle shops and can be added to white and brown breadcrumb powders when you have attracted the fish into your swim. You will need to add very small quantities of bait to the groundbait to hold them there.

Artifical lures are also used and there are vast armouries of plugs, spoons, spinners and mepps spinners available to the angler.

If you are fishing a new water for the first time, use a bait in which you have confidence but also check what other anglers are using. If you don't ask, you won't learn. Be prepared to change your bait or fly. Give your first choice a fair chance but if it isn't working try another. You never know what the fish may want for dinner.

ABOVE Spinning lures for salmon and pike, mepps and tobies.

A Fisherman's Companion

FISHING RECORDS

DATE ....

WATER ....

RODS ....

WEATHER ....

     AIR TEMPERATURE .... WATER TEMPERATURE ....

     CONDITIONS ....

     WIND DIRECTION ....

THE CATCH

FISH ....

....

WEIGHT ....

HOW CAUGHT ....

COMMENTS ....

....

....

....

DATE ....

WATER ....

RODS ....

WEATHER ....

     AIR TEMPERATURE .... WATER TEMPERATURE ....

     CONDITIONS ....

     WIND DIRECTION ....

THE CATCH

FISH ....

....

WEIGHT ....

HOW CAUGHT ....

COMMENTS ....

....

....

44

FISHING RECORDS

DATE ....

WATER ....

RODS ....

WEATHER ....

    AIR TEMPERATURE .... WATER TEMPERATURE ....

    CONDITIONS ....

    WIND DIRECTION ....

THE CATCH

FISH ....

....

WEIGHT ....

HOW CAUGHT ....

COMMENTS ....

....

....

DATE ....

WATER ....

RODS ....

WEATHER ....

    AIR TEMPERATURE .... WATER TEMPERATURE ....

    CONDITIONS ....

    WIND DIRECTION ....

THE CATCH

FISH ....

....

WEIGHT ....

HOW CAUGHT ....

COMMENTS ....

....

....

FISHING RECORDS

DATE ....

WATER ....

RODS ....

WEATHER ....

    AIR TEMPERATURE .... WATER TEMPERATURE ....

    CONDITIONS ....

    WIND DIRECTION ....

THE CATCH

FISH ....

....

WEIGHT ....

HOW CAUGHT ....

COMMENTS ....

....

....

....

DATE ....

WATER ....

RODS ....

WEATHER ....

    AIR TEMPERATURE .... WATER TEMPERATURE ....

    CONDITIONS ....

    WIND DIRECTION ....

THE CATCH

FISH ....

....

WEIGHT ....

HOW CAUGHT ....

COMMENTS ....

....

....

FISHING RECORDS

DATE ....

WATER ....

RODS ....

WEATHER ....

    AIR TEMPERATURE .... WATER TEMPERATURE ....

    CONDITIONS ....

    WIND DIRECTION ....

THE CATCH

FISH ....

....

WEIGHT ....

HOW CAUGHT ....

COMMENTS ....

....

....

....

DATE ....

WATER ....

RODS ....

WEATHER ....

    AIR TEMPERATURE .... WATER TEMPERATURE ....

    CONDITIONS ....

    WIND DIRECTION ....

THE CATCH

FISH ....

....

WEIGHT ....

HOW CAUGHT ....

COMMENTS ....

....

....

....

A Fisherman's Companion

FISHING RECORDS

DATE ....

WATER ....

RODS ....

WEATHER ....

    AIR TEMPERATURE .... WATER TEMPERATURE ....

    CONDITIONS ....

    WIND DIRECTION ....

THE CATCH

FISH ....

....

WEIGHT ....

HOW CAUGHT ....

COMMENTS ....

....

....

DATE ....

WATER ....

RODS ....

WEATHER ....

    AIR TEMPERATURE .... WATER TEMPERATURE ....

    CONDITIONS ....

    WIND DIRECTION ....

THE CATCH

FISH ....

....

WEIGHT ....

HOW CAUGHT ....

COMMENTS ....

....

....

FISHING RECORDS

DATE ....

WATER ....

RODS ....

WEATHER ....

    AIR TEMPERATURE .... WATER TEMPERATURE ....

    CONDITIONS ....

    WIND DIRECTION ....

THE CATCH

FISH ....

....

WEIGHT ....

HOW CAUGHT ....

COMMENTS ....

....

....

....

DATE ....

WATER ....

RODS ....

WEATHER ....

    AIR TEMPERATURE .... WATER TEMPERATURE ....

    CONDITIONS ....

    WIND DIRECTION ....

THE CATCH

FISH ....

....

WEIGHT ....

HOW CAUGHT ....

COMMENTS ....

....

....

....

Gone
Fishing

*In the night I dreamed of trout-fishing; and when at length I awoke, it
seemed a fable that this painted fish swam there so near my couch, and rose
to our hooks the last evening, and I doubted if I had not dreamed it all. So
I arose before dawn to test its truth, while my companions were still sleep-
ing. There stood Ktaadn with distinct and cloudless outline in the moonlight; and the rippling of the rapids was the only sound to break the still-
ness. Standing on the shore, I once more cast my line into the stream, and
found the dream to be real and the fable true. The speckled trout and the
silvery roach, like flying-fish, sped swiftly through the moonlight air,
describing bright arcs on the dark side of Ktaadn …*

HENRY DAVID THOREAU
The Union Magazine (1848)

OPPOSITE *A Young Fisherman*
by Henry John Yeend King, 1855–1924

RIVERS, STREAMS AND CANALS

There is something magical about moving water, from the rushing spring-fed streams which harbour small trout eager to snatch a worm, to the vast salmon pools of the Spey or Wye and the slow-moving rivers of the American South. Every fisherman and woman will have their favourite river, one on which they have enjoyed success and failure.

Where do you fish on a river? Well fish, like humans, like comfortable homes where food is readily available. In fast-flowing streams, fish will rest behind rocks and boulders, in holes under banks, on comfortably placed rocks in the river bed and on the edges of the current where they can easily intercept any flies and insects washed down to them. Watch out particularly for backwaters and eddies. Fish shift their homes when the river rises. The increasing pressure of the water makes them uncomfortable so they move towards the banks and into slacker water.

Some fish, particularly salmon, change their lies in a river according to the time of year and the height of the water. When the water is cold in the spring, they lie in the deeper pools: in the summer they move into faster water. In the

LEFT Trout fishing near Oberammergau, Germany.

autumn, as the spawning urge grows on them, they drop back to the broad gravelly flats at the tails of pools.

In the summer, many fish take cover under beds of weed and emerge at night to feed on gravel shallows. This applies particularly to roach, barbel and chub. Fallen trees and tree roots trap debris and food and always harbour fish. Weir pools are favourite haunts in summer. As well as knowing the habits of the fish, the angler needs to be able to read the water to find the likely places for a taking fish.

The canal is a beautiful place with beds of sedges, luxurious marginal plants, bushes that sometimes kiss the water on the other side, and plenty of bird-life ...

I always fish the lock, letting a small worm down into the deep troubled water, and I generally get a bite or two. If there were any justice in things, one would catch a perch at every visit, but in point of fact I have never caught anything in the lock except chub or dace. Once I hooked a big trout with a fly, and had an anxious time debating how I was to get him out, since my net was too short to reach down to the water, and the lower gates, generally left open, happened to be shut. The trout solved the problem for me by getting off.

H.T. SHERINGHAM

Coarse Fishing (1912)

Canals are a bit different, like rivers but with no current. You can learn where to fish by watching the banks and reed beds, by observing the movement of fish and watching local anglers. Canals are local, personal places.

LAKES, LOCHS AND RESERVOIRS

I love Blagdon, not only because it holds great fish, but because I have always been happy there … (It) is an artificial reservoir, it is true, but it is only the western end that lets you into that secret …You can sit on the grass in a dozen places around the shore and swear you are on the banks of one of the prettiest natural lakes in the kingdom … I know, too, that there was once a witch in the valley and that they drowned her when they let the water in; and one night as I grope my way home in the dark I shall stumble on Hänsel and Gretel asleep on the grass in a mist of white angels, with the myriad million stars of the Milky Way and the golden lights of Blagdon shining on their heads and winking in the watery glass at their feet.

HARRY PLUNKET GREENE

Where the Bright Waters Meet (1924)

LOCHS! – we love the word LOCHS, as applied to those hill-girdled expanses which decorate our native land. Lake is too tame a designation – a shallow epithet. It has nothing to do with mountains and precipices, heaths and forests. Beautiful it may be, very beautiful! Windermere is very beautiful, Derwent water is very beautiful; Buttermere, Ullswater, and Coniston, are very beautiful; for these all lie among hills – but not Scottish hills; not the unplanted places – dwellings of the storm and the eagle.

THOMAS TOD STODDART

The Art of Angling, As Practised in Scotland (1835)

Lakes and reservoirs are another matter. You need to work at them, to fish them continually before you can start to understand where the fish lie and how best to tackle them. A vast expanse of water that you don't know is a daunting prospect. You just have to watch and hope, fish down the shore, off the weir and bank, fish around tree roots and down the side of reed beds. Look out for other anglers, observe where they go. Watch for the bend in their rod to see whether they are having any luck.

ABOVE RIGHT Fishing off the dam, Ladybower
Reservoir, Derbyshire, England.
RIGHT *Fishing on the Lake* by Charles Leslie, 1835-63.

THE ONE THAT GOT AWAY

It is our lost fish that I believe stay longest in our memory, and seize upon our thoughts whenever we look back at fishing days. The most gallant fish when eaten is forgotten, but the fish that after a mad, glorious battle has beaten us and left us quivering with excitement and vexation is hooked and lost again in many years to come.

A.H. CHAYTOR

Letters to a Salmon Fisher's Sons (1910)

Of all the stories that fishermen tell, the most common and least believed is the one that got away. Why, people ask, is it always the very big fish that escaped? Of all fishing stories this is the one most likely to be true. The reason is quite simple. The fisherman, when he hooks a really large fish, is entering an unknown world, a world in which tackle may break under the unaccustomed strain, where lines run out, or where nerves and bungles in landing a monster can cause disaster at the last moment. Most times it is the

angler's own fault. The best advice is don't get impatient when you are playing the fish of a lifetime. Even if you have had the fish on for an hour or more, stay calm, be patient, give it time. The hook hold may wear out, the cast may break, but you will have given yourself the best chance to succeed.

The Fish in the Kitchen (Terms for Carving all sort of Meat at Table)
For Fish; Chine that Salmon, String that Lamprey, Splat that Pike, Sauce that Plaice, and Sauce that Tench, Splay that Bream, Side that Haddock, Tusk that Barbel, Culpon that Trout, Transon that Eel, Tranch that Sturgeon, Tame that Crab, Barbe that Lobster.

HANNAH WOOLLEY

The Gentlewoman's Companion; or a Guide to the Female Sex (1682)

ABOVE A trout coming to a fly.
LEFT *Thursday* by Walter Dendy Sadler, 1854–1923.

FISHING IN WINTER

Fishing in winter may not have the charm of summer, yet there are many possibilities. In the north of Scotland salmon fishing opens on many rivers as early as 12th January, and there is the traditional opening of the season on Loch Tay when the boats set out on New Year's Day. An Atlantic salmon caught in the first months of the year is a great triumph as there are far fewer fish in the river at that time of year; the rivers are clear and cold, swollen with the melting snows from the hills and the weather is often harsh and bitter, so cold that the line freezes to the top ring of the rod.

Many fish reach the peak of their condition in winter – roach, rudd and chub, all of which can prove lanky and spiritless when caught in summer, are often doughty fighters in winter. A fine mild winter's day is best with a full river, bright, sunny and not too cold.

The cream of winter fishing, however, must be for pike. An old fishing saying went "December good, January better, February best"

but even in winter pike fishing is uncertain. You cannot tell in advance what will be a good day, and what a bad one. As with most fishing it just depends on the temperature and where the pike are in their feeding cycle. In rivers, pike fishing will often be good as a flood is clearing or in a mild spell, which may be the harbinger of colder weather. The fascination of fishing for pike in rivers is finding them. Often they lie close in to the banks where they can be caught on deadbaits. A trotted bait, fished just off the tip of the rod, is one of the best ways to explore likely spots. Many pike are caught spinning, often on plugs, which a hungry pike explodes on to in a heart-stopping moment. Perhaps the best way to fish for pike in winter is with the old-fashioned sink-and-draw method. Here the bait is usually a dead herring, roach or dace and it should be swum down the river, free-lined, held over likely spots, allowed to sink to the bottom and then pulled up to the surface, simulating the movements of a dying fish. Do not use too large a bait and strike as soon as the fish is felt.

Early in the morning, while all things are crisp with frost, men come with fishing reels and slender lunch, and let down their fine lines through the snowy field (the frozen lake) to take pickerel and perch …

Ah! those pickerel of Walden! When I see them lying on the ice or in the well which the fishermen cuts in the ice, making a little hole to admit the water, I am always surprised at their rare beauty, as if they were fabulous fishes … They are not green, like the pines, not grey like the stones, nor blue like the sky, but they have, to my eyes, if possible, yet rarer colours, like flowers and precious stones, as if they were pearls …

HENRY DAVID THOREAU
Walden, or Life in the Woods (1854)

ABOVE Fishing for grayling in winter. River Avon, Wiltshire, England.

FISHING IN SPRING

Salmon are now entering the river systems in greater numbers and spring salmon fishing is rightly celebrated as one of the finest of all sports, but in spring the true fisherman fishes for trout.

To enjoy trout fishing to the full you really need to live by a river that you can fish regularly to learn the ways of its insects and fish. Such fishing can provide the angler with a pleasure so intense that it is beyond words.

It was one of those days which May sometimes brings. The sun shone, the sky was blue and silver, the breeze was light and the trees were all of a different shade of green. The water meadows were bright with flowers. The liquid gold of the kingcup was fading, but there were wide drifts of the delicate lilac of the cuckoo flower, whilst in the dryer spots rich yellow cowslips were mixed with the dark purple orchids. The broad Test ran full and fast and stainless. I started at ten o'clock in the morning....

Was this my fish? ...Yes, I suppose it was. I half reeled up, preparing to move on, when a sub-conscious thought forced itself to the front. It said, think again: think of the rise you first saw: picture it in your mind: was that, could it have been, caused by the miserable pounder you have just returned? Think again, it said, and then cast again two yards higher. I lengthened my line, and was rewarded by a rise that made my heart glad. He weighed two pounds and a half.

By now dusk had come on, stars were in the sky and in the air bats had taken the place of swifts. All was over.

... all this entered into the inner chamber of the soul, giving a refreshment, a poise, a balance and a new life to intellect and to emotions which no other experience could offer.

J.W. HILLS

A Summer on the Test (1924)

ABOVE Fishing for trout on a chalkstream in May.

FISHING IN SUMMER

Some fish are associated with summer: bass, crappies, catfish, bream, carp and barbel. Tench fishing is a business of the early morning or the evening when the sun is setting. It needs to be warm and still. Good fish are caught on paste and worms. Catfish too are a fish of the summer. As the water gets warmer, cats get hungrier and baskets full of these fish can be caught by bottom fishing.

However there is no fish that commands the respect of the carp. There are two approaches to carp fishing. There is the reverent approach:

ABOVE *Fishing by a Punt* (detail) by A. W. Redgate.

To him (the carp fisher), when he hears the heavy splash of some big questing carp, there comes a delicious shiver to visit his spine, running up and down it like the flicker of a serpent's tongue. And how many are the noises one hears beside the water at fall of night! Some can be guessed at and mental pictures formed of what manner of creatures they are – others leave one mystified. Nor is the water really still when the sun has gone. Ever and again a ripple passes through the reeds, something patters and squeaks, lily pads stir and shudder, hidden gleams come and go. It is an hour bewitched.

"B.B."
Confessions of a Carp-fisher (1950)

And there is the other approach:

So far as my experience goes, it is certain that good luck is the most vital part of the equipment of him who would seek to slay big carp. For some men I admit the usefulness of skill and pertinacity; for myself, I take my stand entirely upon luck. To the novice I would say: Cultivate your luck. Prop it up with omens and signs of good purport. Watch for magpies on your path. Form the habit of avoiding old women who squint. Throw salt over your left shoulder. Touch wood with the forefinger of your right hand whenever you are not doing anything else. Be on friendly terms with the black cat. Turn your money under the new moon. Walk round ladders. Don't start on Friday. Stir the materials for Christmas pudding and wish. Perform all other such rites as you know and hear of. These things are important in carp fishing.

H.T. SHERINGHAM
Coarse Fishing (1912)

Carp fishing is a religion and the capture of the largest carp is attended by months of patient preparation. It demands dedication, it requires good tackle, for it is the height of folly to fish for carp with inadequate equipment, it needs skill, and most of all, it needs luck.

FISHING IN AUTUMN

The autumn is the best time to catch many coarse or river fish: barbel, roach, dace, chub on a dry fly, perch – many fish at their best. Autumn is also the best time to catch two other fish. One is the grayling which is found in the chalkstreams in the south of England and particularly in the rivers of the Yorkshire dales.

Grayling fishing is as skilled as fishing for trout, and this is the time of the year when they are at their best. A Red Tag is traditionally the best fly to use.

The other fish is the Atlantic salmon, where in October and November the autumn run brings in great fish, leaping upstream over the caulds while the wild duck fly up river and the trees turn golden above the banks.

ABOVE Fishing the Tweedswood Beat, River Tweed, in the autumn.

than at other times. Weather, river and fish seem suddenly to be on the angler's side and prepared to do their best for him. This is not the moment to waste in putting on a fresh cast. Hawthorn trees seem to know this and, joining in the happy conspiracy, skilfully evade the flies that in moments not benign they reach out to clutch greedily behind the angler's back.

ARTHUR RANSOME,
Rod and Line (1929)

There is a blazon of scarlet and gold on the beechwoods that bend to the river. And the reflection of them lies upon the glassy water in a crimson stain. The salmon takes the fly deep down. Calm though it is, his move at me is noticeable only by the slightest humping of the surface – a yard it seems from where the fly ought to be. Then he has it with a straight smooth

The benign moment is difficult to define or explain, though every fisher-man knows it. It is like one of those sudden silences in a general conversation when, in England, we say 'An angel passes' and in Russia, in the old days, they used to say, 'A policeman is being born'. The day is not that day but another. Everything feels and looks different. The fisherman casts not in the mere hope of rising a fish but, knowing that he will rise one, concerned only to hook it when it comes. He knows that even the hooking of it is more likely

pull that takes twenty yards of line along with it. And out he comes with a great sideway wallop, a great red fish to see in the fiery evening and against the golden woods! That is Autumn fishing.

P.R. CHALMERS
Where the Spring Salmon Run (1931)

OPPOSITE Le Ponte de Mantes by Corot (1868-1870).

FISHING RECORDS

DATE ....

WATER ....

RODS ....

WEATHER ....

　　　AIR TEMPERATURE .... WATER TEMPERATURE ....

　　　CONDITIONS ....

　　　WIND DIRECTION ....

THE CATCH

FISH ....

....

WEIGHT ....

HOW CAUGHT ....

COMMENTS ....

....

....

DATE ....

WATER ....

RODS ....

WEATHER ....

　　　AIR TEMPERATURE .... WATER TEMPERATURE ....

　　　CONDITIONS ....

　　　WIND DIRECTION ....

THE CATCH

FISH ....

....

WEIGHT ....

HOW CAUGHT ....

COMMENTS ....

....

....

FISHING RECORDS

DATE ....

WATER ....

RODS ....

WEATHER ....

    AIR TEMPERATURE .... WATER TEMPERATURE ....

    CONDITIONS ....

    WIND DIRECTION ....

THE CATCH

FISH ....

....

WEIGHT ....

HOW CAUGHT ....

COMMENTS ....

....

....

DATE ....

WATER ....

RODS ....

WEATHER ....

    AIR TEMPERATURE .... WATER TEMPERATURE ....

    CONDITIONS ....

    WIND DIRECTION ....

THE CATCH

FISH ....

....

WEIGHT ....

HOW CAUGHT ....

COMMENTS ....

....

....

A Fisherman's Companion

FISHING RECORDS

DATE ....

WATER ....

RODS ....

WEATHER ....

    AIR TEMPERATURE .... WATER TEMPERATURE ....

    CONDITIONS ....

    WIND DIRECTION ....

THE CATCH

FISH ....

....

WEIGHT ....

HOW CAUGHT ....

COMMENTS ....

....

....

DATE ....

WATER ....

RODS ....

WEATHER ....

    AIR TEMPERATURE .... WATER TEMPERATURE ....

    CONDITIONS ....

    WIND DIRECTION ....

THE CATCH

FISH ....

....

WEIGHT ....

HOW CAUGHT ....

COMMENTS ....

....

....

FISHING RECORDS

DATE ....

WATER ....

RODS ....

WEATHER ....

     AIR TEMPERATURE .... WATER TEMPERATURE ....

     CONDITIONS ....

     WIND DIRECTION ....

THE CATCH

FISH ....

....

WEIGHT ....

HOW CAUGHT ....

COMMENTS ....

....

....

DATE ....

WATER ....

RODS ....

WEATHER ....

     AIR TEMPERATURE .... WATER TEMPERATURE ....

     CONDITIONS ....

     WIND DIRECTION ....

THE CATCH

FISH ....

....

WEIGHT ....

HOW CAUGHT ....

COMMENTS ....

....

....

Index